A Tree For Me

Jessica Jaye

SRL Publishing

www.srlpublishing.co.uk

#BreakingTheSilence

SRL Publishing Ltd
42 Braziers Quay
Bishop's Stortford
Herts, CM23 3YW

First published worldwide by SRL Publishing in 2019

ISBN: 978-0995732377

To Papi
A lover of wildlife

If we all plant a tree, imagine what could happen.

There aren't enough words that allow me to thank all those that have helped me with this book.

Thank you to David, my wonderful husband, for helping me to pursue my dreams.

Thank you to Mum for always keeping me motivated.

Thank you to Dad for the feedback and encouragement.

Thank you to my Sister for always being there for me.

Thank you to Zoe Jones, Allyson Cover and Emma Ford for being my first readers.

Thank you to SRL Publishing for making this book a reality.

Sebastian the gibbon is fluffy and long,

with a big smiley face and a happy song.

and lives with his friends
in this beautiful tree.

He would swing through the trees during the day
and meet up with friends to laugh and play.

The sun went down and he was home again

in his beautiful tree all happy, but then...

There was an almighty sound, a bang and a crack
and Sebastian fell with a thud and a smack.

There were lorries and chainsaws ripping down trees. Sebastian watched as he crouched on his knees.

The animals trampled across the hard ground.

Away from the machines and the terrible sound.

Sebastian was sad, he was all alone.

He had lost his friends and even his home.

A little girl came skipping by
and heard Sebastian's tiny cry.

The little girl took Sebastian's hand

and led him towards the golden sand.

She dug a hole that was deep and round

and placed a small seed into the ground.

They covered the seed and watered it too

and watched as the plant began to peep through.

The little girl smiled and skipped away

as Sebastian waited the rest of the day.

Sebastian waited many days and nights,

until he got tired and closed his eyes tight.

While Sebastian slept the tree grew tall,

higher and higher until Sebastian was small.

Sebastian woke and opened his eyes.

The tree was perfect,
he was so surprised.

He jumped up and down, then climbed up high

and sang his song up in to the sky.

His friends heard his call and looked up to the moon.

Sebastian knew they would be home soon.

The animals arrived and looked up at the tree.

They danced with joy and shouted Yippee!

This tree was special, it was everyone's home.

Now no one would ever be left alone.

RAINFOREST
TRUST®

Thank you very much for buying this book. By doing so, you are actively helping to save endangered species and rainforests around the world.

For every copy of *A Tree For Me* we sell, SRL Publishing will make a donation to **Rainforest Trust**, a world-leading conservation charity that protects rainforests and saves endangered species from extinction.

To find out more about Rainforest Trust's important work please visit their website: **www.RainforestTrust.org**.

ABOUT THE AUTHOR

Jessica Jaye is a professional illustrator and qualified teacher from Devon. From her time as a teacher, she found that picture books were a great way to engage young readers but wanted a way to introduce important issues such as deforestation, marine debris and pollution.

After a childhood of finger-painting and copious amounts of glitter, Jess gained a degree in Medical Science before deciding to return to her first passion; art. She currently lives in South Wales where she can usually be found in her studio or hanging out at the local climbing centre.

You can follow her on Twitter @OhJaye

Lightning Source UK Ltd.
Milton Keynes UK
UKHW050758310321
381295UK00003B/22

9 780995 732377